by Mary Stewart

SCHOOL PUBLISHERS

Cover, ©Mario Beauregard/Corbis; p.3, ©Harcourt Telescope; p.4, ©The Granger Collection; p.5, ©Mike Rinnan/Alamy; p.6, ©John Chillingworth/Hulton Archive/Getty Images; p.7, ©Royalty Free/Corbis; p.8, ©Ivan Hunter/Rubberball/Jupiterimages; p.9, ©Royalty Free/Corbis; p.10, ©Eamonn McGoldrick/Alamy; p.11, ©Arnold Gold/New Haven Register/The Image Works; p.12, ©Syracuse Newspapers/The Image Works; p.13, ©Stockbyte Platinum/Alamy; p.14, ©Grace/zefa/Corbis.

Printed in China

ISBN 10:   0-15-377355-3
ISBN 13:   978-0-15-377355-6

Ordering Options
ISBN 10:   0-15-377148-8 (Grade 4 Collection)
ISBN 13:   978-0-15-377148-4 (Grade 4 Collection)
ISBN 10:   0-15-377842-3 (package of 5)
ISBN 13:   978-0-15-377842-1 (package of 5)

2 3 4 5 6 7 8 9 10 0940 17 16 15 14 13 12 11 10 09

Inventors and their inventions can be very fascinating! Inventors will often tinker with their inventions until they are perfect. In this book, we will find out about some amazing women inventors.

Women have been inventing things since long ago. Consider, for example, the work of Hypatia. Hypatia was born in Alexandria, Egypt, in the year 370. She invented the astrolabe, a tool used to measure the positions of the sun and stars.

Obviously, many women have invented things since then. Sybilla Masters, for example, was an American colonist. She lived in the early 1700s and invented a way for corn to be cleaned so that it could easily be used for food. She is considered to be the first American woman inventor.

The patent for Sybilla's invention was given in 1715. A patent means you own the rights to your invention. If you have a patent, no one else can make that invention without your permission. Laws back then did not allow women to own patents, so the patent was issued in Sybilla's husband's name. In later years, women inventors would break through these barriers.

The next time you're riding safely in a car on a rainy or snowy night, you can thank Mary Anderson. She invented the windshield wiper in the early 1900s. Amazingly enough, cars weren't even being made at that time!

Back then, some cities had streetcars. Streetcars were vehicles that rolled through the streets on metal rails. One snowy day, while visiting New York City, Mary took a ride on a streetcar. Snow piled up on the windshield. The driver stuck his head out the window so that he could see where he was going. At that moment, Mary got her idea!

Mary started to work. She soon came up with a "swinging arm." It was made of rubber. The rubber blade would move across the windshield. It would wipe away the snow or rain. The driver of the vehicle would work the blade with a lever. In time, Mary perfected the invention, and it worked!

Mary received the patent for the windshield wiper in 1903. By 1916, all American automobiles had Mary's windshield wipers. Think about all of the cars and trucks on the roads today. There are millions of them all over the world. Almost all of them have Mary Anderson's invention!

Okay, so you don't drive a car. You're not really thankful for windshield wipers yet. Well, here's something that you may have used: liquid correction fluid. That's that white liquid you use to "paint over" any mistakes you make while writing or drawing.

As you may have already guessed, a woman invented it. Her name was Bette Nesmith Graham. Oddly enough, she wasn't even an inventor. She was an office worker. In the years before computers were invented, many things were written using a typewriter. Liquid correction fluid was born because of problems Bette had with a typewriter.

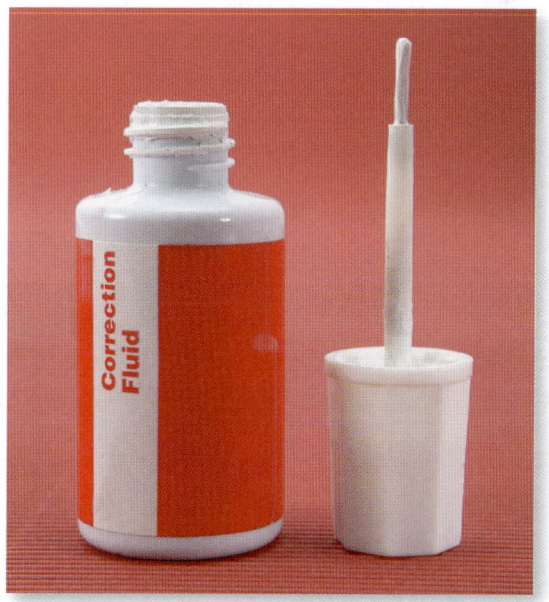

You see, if you spelled a word wrong with a typewriter, it was difficult to correct. You had to use an eraser or, later, a special ribbon to try to erase the word. This usually didn't work very well.

Bette liked to paint. When she made mistakes painting, she just painted over them. She decided to try the same thing with her typing mistakes. She mixed up some white paint and other materials in her blender at home. When she made a mistake typing, she just painted over it with the mixture. It worked!

Soon other workers were using Bette's liquid. In time, she got a patent for the liquid. She started to sell it. Today her liquid correction fluid is used all around the world!

When you trample the carpet with your muddy shoes, your family members probably wish they had some liquid correction fluid to paint over the big mess. Well, if the carpet is protected with Patsy Sherman's product, your family members won't need to worry too much. That's because Patsy invented a special coating. It helps to keep things like carpet clean.

Patsy was working in a laboratory in 1952. She was trying to make a special kind of liquid rubber to be used in airplanes. While working, Patsy accidentally spilled some of the rubber. It landed on a coworker's shoe.

Patsy tried to clean the rubber off the shoe. It wouldn't come off. When she put water on it, the water just rolled right off the shoe. The water wouldn't soak into the rubber or the shoe. She tried cleaners, but those rolled off, too.

Patsy realized this stuff she had made was special. For three years, she worked on the strange liquid rubber. Finally, by 1955, she had made the rubber into a spray that worked just right.

When you spray the product onto a carpet, for example, it forms a "shield." The shield stops water and dirt from getting into the carpet and staining it. The carpet stays clean.

Today, Patsy's product is used on floors, carpets, clothing, and curtains. It's even used on photographs to protect them!

What if you had problems with your eyes?
You'd probably wish for someone to invent a way
for you to see better. Well, that's exactly what a
woman inventor named Dr. Patricia Bath did.

Patricia grew up in Harlem, a neighborhood
in New York City. While studying to be a doctor,
Patricia spent time at a hospital in Harlem. She
saw that many of the people at the hospital had
problems with their eyes. Patricia wanted to help
them. She began to study eyes and how they work.

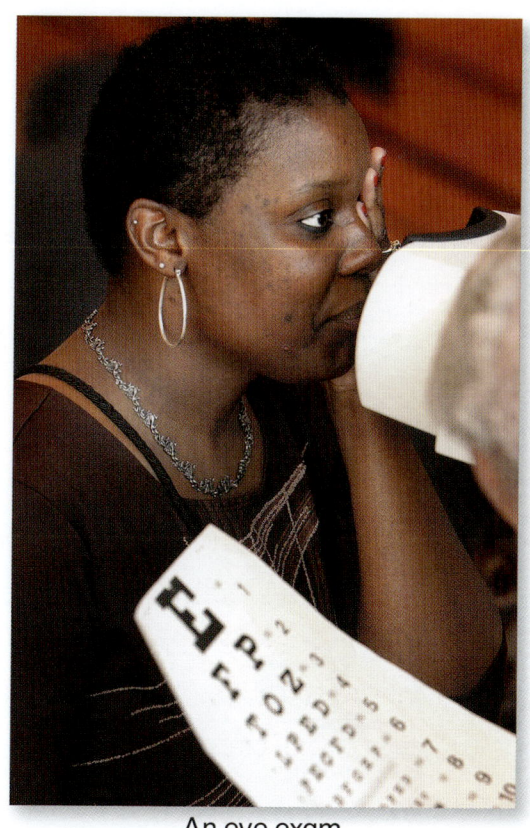

An eye exam

Patricia hoped to find a quicker and easier way to operate on eyes. Her quest began in 1981. She began working with lasers. Lasers are thin, powerful beams of light. Patricia forged ahead. By 1986, she had perfected a laser machine for eye operations. She used it to operate on the eyes of many people. She helped them to see well again!

Today, Patricia's machine is still used. Patricia once said, "The ability to restore vision is the ultimate reward."

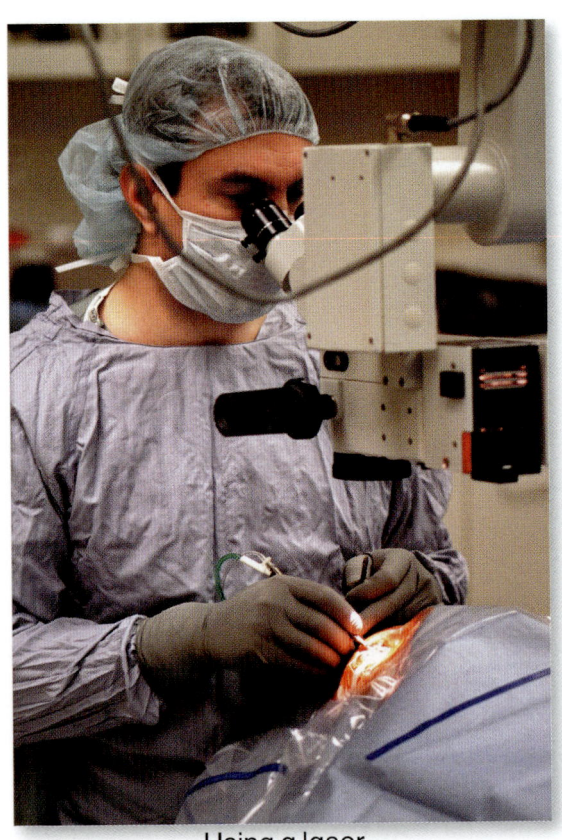

Using a laser

One of the strangest things ever invented by a woman is a self-cleaning house. That's right, it's a house that cleans itself! That means no more dusting or vacuuming. The house does the work for you!

This is no hoax. A house like this actually exists in Newberg, Oregon. A woman named Frances Gabe invented it because she just hated housework!

Each room of the house has a cleaner on the ceiling. The cleaner sprays soapy water into the room, then rinses and dries it. It's like having an automatic car wash in each room of your house. All Frances has to do is push a button, and the rooms get cleaned. Since the furniture is covered with plastic and all the decorations are in glass cases, it does not matter whether they get wet!

Frances's house has other interesting features. Her clothes closet is a washer and dryer. Her kitchen cabinet is a dishwasher. She puts dirty clothes or dishes away, pushes a button, and soon the items are clean—and put away! Now *that* is some awesome invention!

Think Critically

1. Write one fact and one opinion stated in this book.

2. For about how long have women been inventing things?

3. What accident led to Patsy Sherman's invention of a protective liquid rubber?

4. How is Dr. Patricia Bath's invention different from the other inventions described in this book?

5. What did you find most amusing in this book? Why?

 Social Studies

Learn About It Dr. Patricia Bath grew up in the part of New York City called Harlem. Use a research book to find out about Harlem. Write descriptions of three interesting things to see in the neighborhood.

School-Home Connection Discuss this book with a family member. Then have a discussion about other inventions you find interesting.

Word Count: 1,191(1,197)